Avis / Advance Praise for *Ex Nihilo*

« *Ex Nihilo* est un texte sans précédent. Deux grands poètes se répondent, dans un dialogue qui sonde les profondeurs de l'être. On y entend la voix du silence. Cette cantate à deux voix est une merveille, et le miracle qu'est la poésie se produit sur chaque page. » — **Guy Gauthier, New York, auteur de *La Hantise du Passé***

"A poetic meditation on time and existence, *Ex Nihilo* moves like a nebula falling and rising as rhythmic as life-breath itself. The renga spins with the same flow, the same urgency of thought, the same calm, the same passion from one poet to the other, like the perpetual motion of the sea and the wind, like swallows' fluid migrations through time immemorial. At once breath-taking and life-sustaining, *Ex Nihilo* derives from the poets' curiosity and observations about life and death, raising questions-cum-observations in poetic language that scribes the excruciating beauty of transience - of word, of thought, of life. Blodgett and Léveillé produce images out of creation, that linger fragrant, as though in pockets of air in a sun-warm forest, and we understand with them, that breath and words is all there is." — **Karen Clavelle, author of *Iolaire* and *The Mother Goose Letters***

« Ces poèmes exquis à deux voix se succèdent de façon inéluctable, comme le motif d'une fugue de Bach. De toute simplicité, de toute beauté. C'est comme s'ils respirent ensemble, dans un rythme incontournable d'inspiration suivi d'expiration, où chaque souffle est l'expression de la vérité profonde et existentielle qui se révèle dans des phénomènes quotidiens à ceux qui savent voir et écouter : le chant d'un oiseau, une nuit pleine d'étoiles, le bruissement du vent, et enfin le silence... Une œuvre lumineuse dont « la musique des mots » (Verlaine) retentit longtemps après la lecture. » — **Rosmarin Heidenreich, auteure de *Literary Impostors: Canadian Autofiction of the Early Twentieth Century***

"A mighty book, a dive into the sublime, verses grounded in the ethereal present. Code-switching and shape-shifting, lit well yet haunting and entertaining shades, these counterpoint voices exhilarate and grieve, attentive to wonder and perpetuality." — **Renée Olander, author of *American Dangerous* and *A Few Spells***

« Quel recueil émouvant. Sous la forme étonnante d'un renga, ces vers témoignent d'une grande amitié commémorée en images tendres et évocatrices. Un livre unique où magiquement deux voix se font une. C'est un trésor à savourer, à apprécier et à relire. Admirons la virtuosité menée par 'un seul esprit avec deux bouches' de cette inspirante entreprise. » — **Peter Schulman, Professeur de Français et d'Affaires Internationales, Old Dominion University, Norfolk, VA**

Ex Nihilo

AT BAY press

WINNIPEG

Ex Nihilo

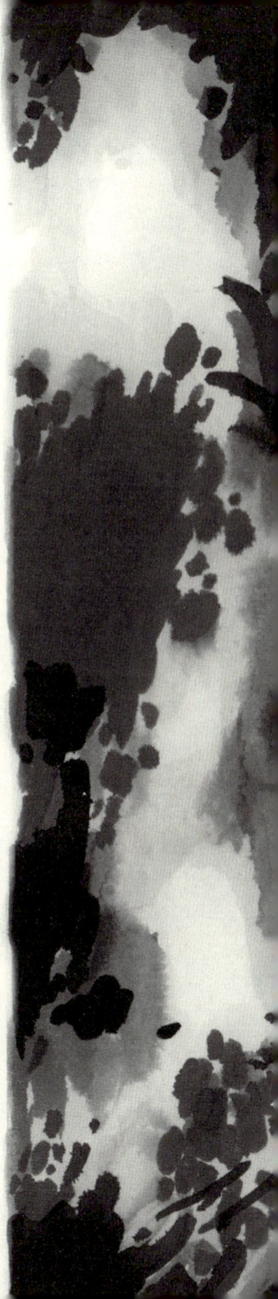

E. D. BLODGETT
J. R. LÉVEILLÉ

Ex Nihilo

Design by M. C. Joudrey and Matthew Stevens.
Layout by Matthew Stevens.

Published by At Bay Press April 2021.

Library and Archives Canada cataloguing in publication is available upon request.

ISBN 978-1-988168-47-0

Printed and bound in Canada.

This book is printed on acid free paper that is 100% recycled ancient forest friendly (100% post-consumer recycled).

First Edition

10 9 8 7 6 5 4 3 2 1

atbaypress.com

Avant-propos / *Foreword*

19 novembre 2018. Je rentre d'un voyage en Afrique. Je songe à écrire à Ted qui n'avait pas communiqué depuis près d'un mois. Je ne le pressais pas, sachant son état de santé plutôt précaire. Il m'avait envoyé, le 18 octobre, son chaînon d'un *renga* (une forme collaborative de poésie japonaise traditionnelle) que nous avions entrepris en 2016 : « J'espère que tu as reçu ma dernière réponse ». Ce fut, en effet, sa dernière. Je lui avais donné réponse le 22 même. Ce maillon clôture notre *renga*.

November 19, 2018. Just back from Africa. I'm thinking of Ted, from whom I had not heard in the past month. His health was fragile and I did not want to rush him into pursuing the renga (a collaborative form of traditional Japanese poetry) we had started in 2016. Ted's response, dated October 18, "Hope you've received my latest reply," turned out to be his last. I had responded on the 22nd, and that poetic link would close our renga.

Ted avait souhaité, à plusieurs reprises, voir publié cet échange poétique, bien qu'il se soit agi à nos yeux d'un *renga* sans fin, écrit par pur plaisir, et j'ai promis d'y veiller. En rentrant au pays, je suis sur le point de lui demander d'en rédiger une préface. Par je ne sais quelle intuition, je suis allé visiter la page Wikipédia qui lui était consacrée.

Là où quelques semaines plus tôt on lisait « is », on trouvait maintenant « was a Canadian poet... »

Pourtant, il le demeure, comme nous l'entendrons dans les pages du poème.

Ted hoped this poetic exchange would, one day, be published, although we both thought of it as an endless renga, written out of pure pleasure – and I promised to see to it. So back in Canada, I was about to write to him asking for a preface. For some unknown reason, I checked out his Wikipedia page. Where a few weeks earlier it had stated "is," the page now read "was a Canadian poet."

Of course he still is, for ever more, as we can see in this poem.

J'ai peu fréquenté E. D. Blodgett, mais je l'ai bien connu par la voie des vers que nous échangions. C'est au tournant du millénaire que j'ai pu voir, pour la première fois, des poèmes en français de sa main. Je lui ai écrit pour lui laisser entendre que les Éditions du Blé sauraient sans doute s'intéresser à ces textes. Il m'a répondu, je crois, qu'il devait d'abord les réserver pour son ami, le poète Jacques Brault. Puis plus rien.

I had not really known Ted before 2016, although I had read some of his work, and came to know him through the voice of the verses we exchanged. Near the turn of the millennium, I had the opportunity to read some French poems of his, and corresponded to indicate that Les Éditions du Blé would no doubt be interested in publishing them. He replied, I believe, that he should first offer them to his good friend Jacques Brault. Then, I heard no more.

Surprise : en 2016, les Éditions du Blé me demandent de rédiger une préface pour un recueil bilingue de Ted intitulé *Horizons* où des diptyques à saveur zen alternent du français à l'anglais. Ce que j'ai fait avec empressement pour en dire toute la beauté et tout le bien que j'en pensais.

Then in 2016, Les Éditions du Blé asked me to write a preface for Ted's Horizons, *a bilingual collection of zen flavoured diptychs alternating between French and English. Which I did posthaste to show all the beauty they contained.*

Ce n'est qu'au lancement du recueil en septembre 2016 que Ted et moi avons fait connaissance. Avec sa moustache un peu hirsute, il me faisait l'impression d'un sympathique morse qui écrivait dans une espèce de code Morse poétique très fin.

I finally got to meet Ted at the launch of Horizons *in September of that year. With his distinctive moustache, he made me think of a great walrus, and of course, he wrote in an exquisite poetical Morse code.*

Le lendemain, nous avons partagé une pizza dans un resto sur les rives de la Rouge. Je l'ai déposé à son hôtel où il m'a demandé d'entreprendre un *renga* avec lui. J'ai dit oui sans hésiter, mais avec beaucoup de réticence – si on me permet la contradiction – car j'ai plutôt l'habitude d'œuvrer en solitaire.

The following day, we shared a pizza at a restaurant on the banks of the Red and I then dropped him off at his hotel. He asked me if I would engage in a renga with him, and I promptly agreed, though with some reservation – if you will allow this contradiction – as I prefer to write on my own.

Quand il me fit parvenir le premier chaînon, le surlendemain – il avait visiblement hâte – c'était parti. Il a lancé le *renga* avec ce vers : *« you spoke of how the wind... »* déclenché, a-t-il dit, par un vers dans mon recueil *Poème Pierre Prière* : « l'ombre du vent ».

Two days later, he sent me the first link of the renga – he was no doubt eager to get going. He started off with "you spoke of how the wind" inspired, he said, by "l'ombre du vent," *a verse from my collection,* Poème Pierre Prière.

Du *renga*, notre suite ne conserve aucun aspect formel. D'ailleurs qu'est-ce que le *renga* sinon le projet de la parole ? Ce recueil en respecte donc la valeur fondamentale : une communication entre deux poètes à travers la poésie l'un de l'autre. Véritablement *à travers*. Et doublement, puisqu'il s'agit, ici, d'un échange bilingue. Au sujet du *renga*, Ted m'écrivait : « Bien que l'on sache qu'un *renga* est une forme dialogique de poésie, c'est une forme très intense où deux esprits deviennent presque un seul esprit avec deux bouches, pour ainsi dire. Puisque un *renga* se compose de chaînons, le défi du poète est double : chaque chaînon doit saisir un élément du poème précédent – une image, une idée, même un mot – et le développer de façon à ce qu'il élargisse ce moment entre deux poèmes, et qu'il s'étende sur le *renga* entier. Donc : écrire un poème qui est à la fois indépendant et qui sert d'entre-deux. »

Our renga retains none of the formalities of the genre. But what is a renga if not the project of its own discourse? This book respects its fundamental value: a conversation between two poets flowing through each other's poetry. Thoroughly throughout. And doubly so, as ours is a bilingual endeavour. On the subject of the renga, Ted wrote: "The renga of course is a dialogical form of poetry, but quite an intense one wherein two minds essentially become one mind with two mouths, so to speak. A renga being composed of successive links, the poet's challenge is twofold: each link must capture a facet of the previous poem – an image, a concept, even a simple word – and develop it in order to expand this conjunctive moment between two poems so that it extends to the entire renga. Therefore, one must write a poem that is independent yet acts as a go-between."

Il me semble que dans *Ex Nihilo*, on trouve davantage de continuité de style chez Ted. Ou disons plutôt, lui en harmonie, moi en contrepoint ; lui plus concentré, moi plus insouciant.

It seems to me that in Ex Nihilo, *the reader will find more continuity in Ted's stylistic approach. Or let us rather say, he in harmony and I in counterpoint; Ted more concentrated and I slightly more insouciant.*

Je ne puis dire précisément comment il fonctionnait – certainement avec doigté, sagesse et grande circonspection. Pour ma part, je lui ai avoué avoir parfois « triché », c'est-à-dire avoir eu recours, deux ou trois fois, à d'anciens poèmes ou passages, car ils semblaient tout à fait appropriés à notre suite – espèce d'auto-plagiat par anticipation. Mais c'est ma façon, et cela ne lui a pas déplu.

I cannot attest to his process – certainly he proceeded with finesse, discretion and great understanding. I, on the other hand, admit having occasionally "cheated," in the sense that I reinserted, on two or three occasions, past poems or passages as they seemed so appropriate to the sequence – a kind of anticipated self-plagiarism. It is how I roll, and Ted did not seem to mind.

À l'occasion, certains courriels se sont croisés et nous avons eu deux suites pour un même chaînon, alors j'ai carrément changé l'essor, mais toujours dans l'esprit du texte, et tout cela a été intégré en son temps.

A few times, our emails crossed paths and we would end up with two sequences for the same link. I would then clearly sound a different note, always within the spirit of our renga, and all was integrated in due course, to our satisfaction.

Certains décèleront peut-être chez Ted la trace, tenue assez coite, de sa lutte contre la maladie. On s'imagine à quel point l'écriture pouvait lui être un baume et une nourriture. C'est Ted qui a proposé *Ex Nihilo* comme titre de ce *renga*, que nous avons retenu. Il est à point.

Some may detect in Ted's verse a slight trace, always held hushed, of his struggle against illness, and one can readily imagine the extent to which writing was an energizing balm. Ted suggested Ex Nihilo *as the title of this renga, which we have retained. It is spot on.*

Enfin, j'aimerais en mon nom, et celui de Ted, remercier Matt Joudrey de At Bay Press d'avoir si bien veillé à la réalisation de ce projet de la parole poétique, et je suis personnellement reconnaissant qu'il ait voulu ainsi rendre hommage à un merveilleux poète, E. D. Blodgett.

Finally, I would like to thank, in Ted's name as well, Matt Joudrey of At Bay Press, for having so beautifully conceived this bilingually poetic project, and I thank him, personally, for having rendered a lasting homage to a marvelous poet, E. D. Blodgett.

J.R.L.

you spoke of how the wind
had certain shades

curtains of
the lengthening afternoon

infinity falls slowly through
the late light

le vide prend la forme qu'il veut
et tout ce qui vient va

je reste en place
pour l'éveil de la nuit

waking in the dark
as if one were asleep
inside a tree

so near the breath of leaves
their slow music unfolding
and the stars

on oublie que la nuit
poursuit sa descente
jusqu' à la levée du jour

bruissement dans les hauts bois
un orchestre de rien du tout

of all oboes merely one
standing in the emptiness
of clouds

a single note unheard
that gathers all endlessness

o breath
that makes of this
immeasurable of everything that is

the is that is

je n'écoute plus la musique du clavecin
le luth me suffit

je n'écoute plus la mélodie du luth
l'oreille me suffit

« tout ce que je vois, je l'entends
tout ce que j'entends, je le vois »

sans aucun motif

birds departing across
the darkness of the sea

their wake
cries they make
calling to the moon

and everywhere upon the sea
fragments of the moon

birds singing in their absence
gathered by small moons
their music playing lightly over waves

qui perce la ténèbre
étoiles ou oiseaux ?
les uns la pointe de la nuit
les autres le point du jour

ceci se dit aussi
jouer du luth sans corde

la lune parfois se lève
où le soleil se couche

as one who stands
upon the surface of the sea
no land in sight

dissolving so swiftly that
the least of things are
without compass under the sky

here the sun and then the moon
begin their slow rise

where to turn
what question to be asked

dans le lit du vent
toute dérive m'est indifférente

léger comme plume
j'émerge du vide de la vague

son volume ne répond à aucun son
ne suit aucun tracé
ne s'arrête à aucune forme

when emptiness arrives
all its past slipping by

nothing of what was
remaining near

if it were waves
or smaller stones upon a shore

or birds their ghosts trailing off

or emptiness that waits
to come again

a child gone blind

comment dire
ce qui semble indicible

pourquoi aller
où il n'y a pas plus de place
à être
rester pour ne point avancer

l'illusion se lève toujours
sur un autre mirage

ce qui paraît vraiment
chuchote

the merest rustling under leaves
a squirrel perhaps
a breath of air lost

a nestling in the mind
where the small feet of squirrels
never arrive

a naked sound
where moons rise
and smaller stars

sufficiencies of breath
the keeping of a world
barely heard

puis il y eut un vent terrible
mais le vide
n'était pas le tourbillon

il y eut un tremblement
mais le vide
n'était pas dans ce séisme

il y eut un feu
et ce qui disparaît
n'était pas dans le feu

puis il y eut un souffle léger
et rien d'autre n'occupa la place

que ceux qui ont des oreilles
entendent

someone singing
as day disappears
ombra mai fu

the music falling
as slowly as
a slow autumn of leaves

so nothing falls
and with it falls
snow falling from stars

the nothing that exhales
the quick invisible
of birds sighing in the dark

parfois faut-il écrire
à travers son ombre

point d'origine

the absent air
where birds have passed

nothing to see
seeing nothing

seeing the past
of small birds

palimpsest
for koto and harp

où est passé l'oiseau ?

le moineau s'envole
avec ses voyelles

il arrive sans se retourner
repart sans s'annoncer

j'avance sans résider
j'abrite ce qui n'a ni toit
ni demeure

nothing covers us
but open sky

the wind caressing us
caressing stars

what is longing but
the sound that sparrows make

giving air the space
where trees stand up

and all that breathes
draws in its life

all longing but
brief shelters exhaled

vent vide voie
puis-je dire
autrement

si tout se tait
demeure un reste

la voix
n'aspire à rien
inspiration
expiration

from nowhere like
snow combing through winter air

or auroras
whispering against the sky

rise up cries the rose
and grass in quickened gasps

what is silence but
the shape music takes

the least stone that holds in sleep
all that was and is not yet

la ligne qui avance
n'est pas celle qui précède
elle n'a jamais suivi

elle procède
entièrement

of geese
where journeys begin
turning above the highest tree

what skies await
what coasts where seas
mindless rise and fall

and what mind is theirs
of geese in their endless turning

what mind the sun's
what mind of long departures
and returns

the turning itself
the mind without thought
a sphere

where what there is eternal
turns

a tree
the sole compass of the world

ciel
silence
le cri
des galaxies

« you want it darker
we kill the flame »

what are these final stars
that softly burn behind
the edges of the universe

their ashes drifting slowly past
the naked planets
the flocks of startled birds

to pause here without a word
but for these
that hold their fall

words that are
the place where stars appear
the eyes of children open in the dark

soyons juste
ce qui est
et qui n'est pas
sera

chaque oiseau
a sa branche
tous les chants
leur note
l'enfant son heur
le temps son retour

le silence
dans la dissolution
s'étend
tempo
sans merci

the same for soldiers in a field
or children by the sea
the sun is without pause

la belle dame
of infinite time

nothing but
the coming and the going of the light

who can weep her passing
who knows the sorrow that she knows

all of them falling through her eyes
soldiers cut down
falling flowers of children

the long winds
heliotropic and round

qui veut la paix
prépare la guerre
la phrase dort
tranquille
deux-points rouges
au côté droit

sur tous les rivages
à travers les nuits
flottent les fantômes
des grands héliotropes

a sentence that
like birds traced on paper
turning till it seems to end
where two bills meet

if someone were to cry out
the sound that would be heard
would be a sound going round
at each turn an echo of eternity

where the centre is
two phantoms that appear as one
rising in its transparency
the is the sentence is

peut-on entendre le son
d'une seule main qui écrit ?

ouïe !

Van Gogh s'empresse :

à Théo
ici stop arrive
stop poésie

at noon the sun
unable to remain the sun alone
burst

where it fell
shards sprang up in flower
beyond sight

no letter can
contain them nor
word state their shape

silence open
silence un-
disclosed

Van Gogh se tranche
l'oreille pour mieux voir

Bodhidharma se taille les cils
car il a soif

le vide :
je me tais
le vent :
pour parler

Bouddha de neige
où sont les neiges d'antan ?

snow falling
but only in its memory falling

it is eternity that falls
falling through a single ear

alone attuned
to music of the snow

no one steps here
without becoming that place

where planets and the sun
are the one music heard

les palmes font signe
sans signifier
ombre du balancement
de l'air

menus coquillages
un univers

le rêve s'éveille sans cesse

as one struck blind
walking without thought
upward toward the sky

nothing but blue air
the sound that falls so blue
from tracks of small shells

and one might raise a hand
to wave against the light
blue the only sound

the sound of endless dreams
waking in the light
ears singing of blue

poisson bleu. yeux bleus. tout bleu.

il n'y a pas de topologie du cœur
l'âme non plus n'a de géographie
pourtant l'esprit traverse
l'univers comme une histoire

plumes de boa dans la marine du ciel
« mer mêlée au soleil »
que me reste-t-il ?

stopping beside
an unknown road

admiring hills
the foreign flowers

the late light
of the sun gone

no after yet
and no before

silence falls
between words

silence where
the light remains

eternity
wakes alone

où je vais
le temps
est là

immense
simple
vide
radieux

je me tais
tout est dit

as one who stands beside the sea
water rising and falling
the sound it makes without end

as one who hears infinity
unable to speak a word
that is not drowned and washed away

as one at last spoken through
every syllable
the sea that speaks and passing birds

as one who speaking is the sea
its waves the only word
the sea exhaling time's breath

le vent est la voix
du vide qui apparaît

la vague
espace du temps

je suis
ce souffle

or so
sitting under willow trees

their leaves waving
under the summer wind

if waking comes
the trees may be gone

taking the wind in
breath is all there is

sur le porche de la saison
mon vieux balai
la pluie tombe
rien à balayer

ce que j'aspire est musique...
j'expire dans un transport
qui a forme de nuages

beside the moon
a cloud without rain

and on the cloud
the smallest birds sang

this is where
ending does not arrive

the phases of the moon
placing cloud and birds

luna lunera

crépuscule du soir
crépuscule du matin
le croassement des corneilles
est-il invitation au voyage
ou dernière note de la symphonie

tout se dissipe
dans le blanc nuage du rêve
étoile du soir étoile du matin

la lumière se jette
où elle peut
petit boson
dit beauté

an angelus of voices that
rise upon the summer dusk

low in the west
the evening star stands

before its light
the darkness disappears

the light that falls
unerring in the heart

voices rising to meet its fall
beginnings and the end

voices and the light
immeasurable embrace

ce qui ne se mesure pas
est compris
ce qui est indicible
se trouve dit

le chœur bat
sans chercher de voie
« ... heureux qui comme Ulysse... »

le temps file
et il est toujours là

Ulysses alone
sitting at the ends of the earth
with birds their flights given up

where the young moon
breathes its slow auroras
reflecting on the sea

and rising in his gaze
its silhouette forever new
"It was Ulysses and it was not"

the moon impossible to grasp
the shape of time
the light alone of night

de tous les temps
la lumière

de toutes les grâces
celle des dieux
la ténèbre
nie les ténèbres

Hamlet danse
sur la tête d'une épingle

a tree stands
just to say *tree*

the wind speaks
merely speaking itself

the universe if asked
can only answer yes

nothing turns
more swiftly than

angels when they dance
becoming all turning

surrender of
the deepest seas

breath
all that grace can be

ce qui va
vient et
revient encore

les chants connus
vont de branche en branche

tout ce qui passe
repasse

sons des cuivres
dans le décor de l'été

ce qui est fête
ce qui devient

the portals of the sun
exhale the great light

birds explode
the colours of banners in a storm

and stones clap hands
at the swift coming of the stars

what was lost
now returns

everything forgotten
now stands beside you

all desire
rests upon your hands

the dead at peace under trees
roses spilling from their eyes

le sable millénaire d'un galet
n'est que galaxie explosée

les éphémères ont leur durée
les lucioles leur nuit

mouche mouche à feu
mouche à miel

donnez-moi pour terre
le ciel
la mémoire
à l'horizon des événements

for God the stars
inside the fog
sing like fireflies

murmurs of joy
rising from his childhood
ring the universe

filling the sound of snow
before it falls

quand Dieu était enfant
il dessina que son dessein
était l'enfant

il dessina dans les circonstances suivantes :
il avait de l'encre
et du papier qu'il dessina

and all of us
content to walk on paper
beneath an origami sky

nothing
the sun the stars the moon
not enfolded there

each unfolding through
every layer of time

the smallest stone
floating up into the sky
becoming moon

through all the skies
where folds of the universe
undulate together

at play invisible
the hands of God

la rivière du temps
coule dans son propre lit
c'est peut-être le lit du vent

ce souffle va où il veut
et quand il vient
il revient

je marche sur l'eau du ciel
on voit les plis de mon papier
onduler

as if the wind
riffling over the sea

the wind and not the sun
in broken exhalations

were the only time
where each of us

comes and goes
with no more sound

than waves
rustling like paper

replis du temps
sur les rives écrites

qui va là ?
qui s'engendre

chaque page d'écumes
chaque ligne
d'une douce exhalaison
chaque mot
aspire à expirer

leafing through
the pages of a book
the words exhaling dust

and late summer afternoons
without a breeze
the poplar leaves whispering

"Alles ist Blatt"
and we but fractals
uttering what is left

steigerung
métamorphose en aval
en amont
contraction en expansion

Rome n'a pas été créé
en un jour pourtant
toutes les routes y mènent

ikh bin az ikh bin
variations sur un thème

if leaves
then paper breathes

all the marks that it consumes
coming back
the same and not the same

where then do waves fall
but on the heart's shore
each diastolic pause
the inspiration of

the all we are

bruissements brisures
au repos
le souffle s'épuise
à se dire
et dans son dict
toute feuille s'évapore

la plume « ne se meut
ni dans le lieu
où elle se trouve
ni dans le lieu
où elle ne se trouve pas »

a feather set free
upon the air
how to speak of it

one note perhaps
in counterpoint
a moon taking shape

within the mind
almost

or just the mind
thinking what it is
its thoughts always

on the point
of falling apart

sur le point de
mettre un point
la plume retourne
au commencement

première note
à l'initiale
l'esprit s'égaye
de se retrouver

slow music
of all rain
and leaves
and snow

falling
da capo
through the universe

the naked aleph
of rain
its long anagoge
never reaching ground

pluies et chants
neige et manège
l'encre en ascension

la feuille remonte
à la branche
papillons de mots

tout tourne
autour

al fine
je reprends (bis)

all sleep
a waking then

the world given only to
the blind

to seek the way to light
walk further into dark

home is the heart
that beats and then retreats

blanc pur
la page

blanc les vagues
de la lune

blanc l'encre
qui sait disparaître

blanc de ténèbre
le silence qui chante

blanc léger les voiles
du cœur

transparent le pouls
de rien du tout

what whiteness waits
in the hand of God
when all that's white

drifts forth

a whiteness that is not
a colour but
the dream of whiteness

known to lovers alone

the breath of white roses
rising into summer nights
of snow exhaled

blanche blancheur
plus transparente
que l'étalement du vent
plus légère
que l'arrivée du sommeil
plus diaphane que l'éveil
plus indicible que le souffle
« l'absente de tous bouquets »

the innerness of white
sits inside eternity
a bare seed
before being

all that will be known
a white thought
poised without thinking
in the mind of God

a logos seed
that sings in silence
a seed that springing open
falls as snow invisible

all that is
flowers of that snow
the ground left behind
the ground that waits ahead

clé de sol
nuages de neige
dans l'encre bleue

le rien du vide
né en verbe

falling between
"the nothing that is not there
and the nothing that is"

all alphabets
and shadows of the birds
that have not been

following wakes
of anagrammatic stars
through the skies

une étoile s'étiole
feu feu
funérailles d'éclat
dans le temps déjà tu

le ciel est aussi lisse
que la tapisserie d'Hélène

« l'ombre de l'oiseau qui vole
ne bouge pas »

so in the highest winds
shadows remain
unperturbed

as if
Plato himself exhaled
and thoughts as shadows stood

unruffled in his breath
holding up
the frailty of stars

dans la caverne
toute ombre est une bénédiction
mais la poésie n'est pas admise
dans la cité

l'enfant de saint Augustin
s'empresse à verser la mer
dans l'enlisement de la pensée

lying down
upon the sill

what saints have passed here
the air passing them
mere music

the moon is so near
they may have touched it
hands the shape of longing

"Weh mir, wo nehm' ich, wenn
Es Winter ist, die Blumen"

est-ce la bénédiction de l'eau
ou la rose des vents
qui fait l'air du temps ?

soleil et ombre
« pauvre étoile au nom miraculeux »

is it the name
the star
or wind rose

that is the miracle

the sun
"l'être en majesté"
etched upon the sky

« toutes choses ont nom
lumière et nuit »

ce qu'on nomme
apparaît
ce qu'on tait disparaît

l'unique trait de pinceau
est sans origine

going is
where coming was

so petals from
the cherry trees
fall to dust

when fires go out
where is out

ô os
ossement
que hante la cendre

tant de ciels
sous d'autres encore abolis

vertèbres de nos voix
ivres toujours
d'astres vifs

like the rest
of an eternal snow
fragments of bones

scattered under all
the prairie earth

remembering us
the o's of ossuarian oboles
cast at random here

what destiny
abolira the rolling bones

tu dis : « et nous, les os,
devenons cendre et poudre
... plus becquetés d'oiseaux
que dés à coudre »

pourtant
la fortune n'est pas
une fatalité

la dérive du destin
est-elle décidée ?

fatum cubitum
dans l'articulation
de mes vers

the fine threads
of autumn mornings
drifting in the sun
their canny makers waiting

how much finer
lines of music
falling from the planets
where we all are enmeshed

no bird entrances so
how eagerly we yield
dancing with the universe
no more are we than this

destiny is not a law
or fall of gravity
it is merely who we are
were we so fortunate to fall

l'été a été
et je me réveille en rêve
l'orbite de l'œil
dans la gravité de sa ténèbre

je veille dans mon sommeil
à entendre le chant des oiseaux
pure ligne de leur émoi

je ne dénombre pas le temps
« I can't keep track of each fallen robin »

a singer
standing on the nearest edge
sings and hears
the silence of each cadence

and birds
the contrapuntal breath of silence
hear and sing
their harmonies unheard of

no tempo for
the time that each keeps
each silence strung beneath
other suns and other darkness

gazing over the sea
unnumbered eternities keening past

la voix n'est pas le verbe
les poumons ne sont pas le souffle

il faut sortir du paradis
pour parler comme des dieux

mémoire des sons
dans l'opéra du cosmos

la ligne replie
sa partition
vierge de toute éternité

to be of paradise
breaths going out

or tears
like showers among stars

or purities asleep
that "lie immortal in the arms of fire"

et « après le feu le bruissement
d'un souffle léger »

je suis prêt seigneur
pour les étoiles du firmament
les eaux des quatre fleuves
et même la flûte de Pan

qu'Aphrodite m'emporte
qu'Athéna me protège
je donne aux muses
mon corps

tout Archimède ne pourra déplacer
une note de Pythagore

the last mythology
is where the mind
begins to burn

a salamander full
of God

no fingers but
candles that
kindle stars

l'attente est impossible
dans les cendres

la plume du phénix
fixe ce qui toujours
s'en va

dieu rampe dans l'éden

of all final gestures
nothing is so firm
as a phoenix up in flames

as if God himself
were in the fire
and smoke his last breath

and all prayer ash
God upon his knees
growing silent

the feathered fall of smoke
filling the void that God
leaving leaves

each prayer
echo of the Logos
speaking the phoenix again

and again
the ash
that flutters in the wind

les cendres seraient-elles
le corps du vent ?

la chevelure d'Absalom
la toile d'araignée ?

ce qui est mortel
médusé ?

Dieu est la disparition
qui accroche

clinamen des âges

a swerve that is
without age

its inside
the Word that God
may have spoken

breath
its holiness
taken unawares

a catch in the throat
left behind

dans le pli et le repli
entre le faste et le néfaste
le vers et le revers
jour et nuit se livrent
en échange de mots

le destin n'est pas fatalité
la fortune chance

not fate or chance
the moon rises

in darkness

its light
always but never
the same

it floats
over the sea
playing with the water

turning providential tides
that breathe
in and out

l'orbe en son orbite
plume légère
« sur l'océan des âges »

soumise insoumise

la providence est prodigue
l'enfant aussi

le fils revient
comme il est parti

dans toutes les complaisances

the smallest stone
thrown into pond
transformed into

circles that
ripple wider and wider
until they lap

on the shores of stars
Sufis inside the sun
whispering *o*

au commencement
la fin me suffit

dix mille mares
dix mille lunes
le vent

the wind alone
enough

everywhere
invisible

the end
without end

stirring
in darkness

de moins en moins
le vide n'est rien

seule la voix
seul le passage
de la voie
issue d'elle-même

inside the whirlwind
what speaks

inside the burning bush
what laughs

and what words
scattering seeds

that parse the stars
the bare planets

mere voice
where the sun sleeps

parler la parole
si aucun mot ne suffit

taire ce qui est tu

standing on
the highest roof you call
to the sun

how can the sun know
that you are calling
and why

all the sun can know
are all the words
you say

each word is you
take the roof
away

whatever speaks
the listening sun is you
in silence

puis...
retour à l'origine

je mets la voile sur la nuit
l'infini chatoiement du vent
devenu l'astre de ma parole

Icare sans ailes

when the voice
first uttered the universe
stars fell

into the fresh dark

the origin
rising through itself
its veil of wings

silence surprised

de crépuscule en crépuscule
l'aube précède l'aurore
et la tombée décline

le blanc vide s'inscrit
à l'horizon de la ligne
chrysalide des nues

perhaps the only sound
was broken glass
that no one heard

a glass silence
that lay between
nothing and the rest

crystal chrysalis
broken into grass
the lonely trees

music of rain
and emptiness
the angelus of margins

comète commise
à sa trace éblouie
marge fuie
dans l'éclat
et dans la nuit

« tantum ergo sacramentum »

what surprised god
strays on the leaping margins

seeds of a cosmos
raining from his hands
tanquam mons magnus igne ardens

ni mont ni tempête
ni buisson ardent
un léger bruissement

tout ce que vous entendez
vous le voyez

dites ceci
en mémoire de moi

what ancient logos
like the phoenix sleeps
upon your tongue

fires of birth and death
have no fears for him

singing all
that can be lit by song

l'oiseau du tonnerre
sépare les eaux d'en haut
des eaux d'en bas

Quetzalcoatl resplendissant
ne parle pas une langue fourchue

ce qui rampe aux pieds d'Ève
serait-il oiseau de paradis ?

comme l'oiseau-mouche et sa fleur
le dragon chinois écrit

de droite à gauche
de haut en bas

avec l'encre des cendres

ce qui se dit
l'ombre de l'ombre

farewell
all the prancing gods
the fallen thunder
apocalypse
of memory and fire

we remain
ashes falling from our mouths
recalling all
the great creation
its beginnings

unfathomable
its long unfolding
floating on the faded smoke
a reveille of birds
sarabandes awakening the world

terre rouge
de la Rivière-Rouge
grande bouche du Manitou
le lieu de dieu est nulle part
adam avant adama
je suis que je suis

lo I
that playful eye
crying aye
across the sky

a sly word
that sighs bird

le corbeau
a la plume facile

le vent a le corbeau

pour dessiner le vent
il suffit de prendre la plume

all the winged words
taking flight

the waves of murmurations
laying out a universe
invisible

enough to be
spoken

the breath of it
exhaling
plummeting stars

mon souffle se coupe
à même le firmament
quand le couteau
détache les pages

soupir et respir
pour donner au vers
le dernier mot

as if
all space recoiled
the moon breathless
between two musics
where *a* at home appeared but as
an exhalation beyond hearing
unspoken star

heaven
the book
where everything *existe pour aboutir*
springs apart

« dans des circonstances éternelles »
a est b n'est pas c

le vide est rien

nothing
or nothing at all
emptiness is where
a solitary bird

beyond all seeing
sings of what
no one has heard
before

oiseau
toutes les voyelles emportées

est-ce assez ?

when is enough
ever enough

spring desires
the summer sun

autumn longs
for winter sleep

perhaps for Orfeo alone
coming back from hell

quelle fable
que cette montée
et cette descente !

qui suit la flûte de Pan
tisse un long voyage
au fil d'Ariane

tangled in Ariadne's hands
threads of yarns darkly lie

where *la diritta via era smarrita*
string theory spinning out

la route qui monte
est la même qui descend

Tityre couché à l'horizon
chante les événements

de l'enfer au paradis
la voie se purge d'elle-même

Tityrus walking through
the slow shades of time
asleep and not asleep

holding his oaten pipe
and singing of the stars
each rising in dream

how punctual the stars
the sky that fills his dream
falling through his eyes

Tityrus in ecstasy
walking where God walks
dreaming where God dreams

Dieu qui rêve est lui-même un songe
aussi éphémère que mouches à feu

Tityre a les yeux de bouc
Dante des yeux de chat

Shitao dessine les yeux fermés
au cœur du cyclone

a fan opens
slow farewells
rising over the sky

distant thunder written on
forgotten margins
the smell of ferns unfolding

against a rainy sky
a small boat will pass
only its absence visible

a fan opens
entre tes mains sans paresse
silence asleep in your hand

opens

entre toast et éventail
le temps sans presse

plis et replis
des feuilles mobiles

l'idée du vent
transparence unique
et unanime
balaie et Charon
et l'Achéron

the waters lift and fall
a sea but not a sea
where all creatures disappear

only to return
as birds come back
upon their rivers of air

the waters breathe
beneath the tidal air
all creatures of the moon

ver purureum
floating down to hell
overflowing with flowers

Ô solstice vernal
soleil pourpre de pluie
pétales de fleurs emportées
loin des flots
sur un air de flûte
berceau de tous les chants
et de tous les oublis

o meadows of asphodel
forgotten light of the sun
Persephone filled
with longing for the spring

all of it afloat
on leaves of asphodel
their petals falling like ash
against *the nothing that is*

« serions-nous donc déjà parvenus au naos » ?

il n'y a pas de dieux en enfer
quoiqu'en disent Hadès et Perséphone
personne pour faucher le pré

les anges de l'éden ne gardent rien
les lis des champs ne peinent ni ne filent

allons gratuitement

boys astray upon a beach
gathering shells
lifting all the echoes of the gods
high against their ears

shells speaking in tongues
never heard before
all the heavenly worlds
asleep in the emptiness of breath

dans la conque l'origine
verbe quantique émis
en spirales

l'enfant verse la mère
dans le sable galactique

sprindrift over sand
the seas spill and stars
mere mirrors of
the whirling world

o merle lilting in the sun
the spell you cast
that lifts sea and star
sine syllabis temporum

les anges chantent
sans orthographe

Kronos apparaît
a tempo

mach 1 à 5
a e i o u

a hush falls at dusk
as if all the stars
speak across the sky
rising from one breath
of bright calligraphy

spoken into light
all the letters in code
the whispering of angels
the hush of nightfall
l'etterno del tempo

·

dans toute allégorie
la comédie

tant pis
pour le tempo

ante Dante
« had a great fall »

antidote
à tant de temps

cranes against the moon
music played on glass
what is the time that was

a hand that waves at dawn
a hand that waves at dusk
what is the time that was

beauty without light
flags on the ground
what is the time that was

Philip Glass écoute
encore et encore

Steve Reich compose
vite moins vite vite

John Cage
fait coucou

Meredith Monk gueule
Ah ! Euh... Hi ! Oh ? Hue !

le chat s'étire :
« Oui, je vois l'heure ; il est l'Éternité ! »

as if a universe
opened for a moment
its large eye

and light into darkness fell

a darkness that is
the silence of light
a light that rises in the eye

as music is remembered

the darkness and the light
the light that utters *tacet*
the darkness that takes it away

l'œil de l'éternité
n'a pas la vision fixe

les yeux sont deux
alors que Tout est Un

taire ce qui est tu
n'est ni parole ni silence

ponctuation
par oscillation

a field of fireflies
floating in your hand
their hearts beating the light

exfoliating eden
without the snake and tree
no voice in the air

a genesis
signalling itself
brief auroras flicking on the dark

luxure des libellules
lumière des lucioles
les hirondelles
à tire d'aile
dans d'autres ciels

luxe de ma vie
quand la lune
est en latence

of the planets
no necessity
carries them

the clear call of bells
filtering the air
of memory

mirrored on the sea
the slow light
of all the air

la gravité
a sa propre orbite

tout est léger
dans l'air du temps

souffle parfait
inodore incolore
et sans saveur

la mémoire tinte
quelque part au Tibet

a mind of cats
dreams in the sun
distilling afternoon

a solitary note
opening air
and trees stand up

a young moon
leaning back on the wind
gravity gone

le chat s'étire
dans le séjour du sphinx

méandre de la nuit
de midi à minuit

œil d'ombre sur l'étang

la lune accompagne le vent

the wind where all our prayers
rise up
before they are
dispersed

returned as what
we could not think to be
the prayers now
praying us

a light rising from
the fresh ash of stars
shades of the phoenix's fire
unforeseen moons

parole est prière
souffle indicible du vent
apparu dans le feu
dont la cendre signe
le plus bel oiseau

fantômes de lunes
dans l'écho d'une naïade

the dust
of niaids passing

the breathing moon

the wake of a bird

memories of bells
incense over the sea

eau azur
ciel marine
votre battement léger
ou turbulent
emporte l'angélus des rêves
qui se mirent dans la crête
de vos vagues nuages

deep cerulean blue petals
falling from the dahlias across
nocturnal skies

a dusty blue
that drifts over the seas

becoming the dusk

lifting the stars
into their deeper firmaments

cerulean cosmos of dahlias
their colour given up
nodding farewell to the sun

les nuages dessinent
une silhouette gitane

le cormoran bleu
au grand cœur noir
valse sur l'illusion de l'air
et de l'eau

la mer de la nuit
se replie – vocables
d'atome

le temps est révolu
c'est certain

at last the atoms speak
their syllables leaping into
the early air
the sounds they make
of children in their glee
flung over the sea
the air invisible
screeching with cormorants

genesis
a gypsy spinning into time

vagues
et volutes de vagues
l'enfant enfonce une mer
dans l'encrier :

fin de la genèse
les oiseaux de l'apocalypse
se taisent
tout maintenant
est appelé à paraître
et disparaître
dans la jouissance
atomique du souffle

what can rise
from silence
the clamour of apocalypse
gone

what can rise
from where the child
writes the first word

just beyond hearing
the slow breathing
of a universe
makes its first gasps

bursting apart
through patient
bright millennia

ce qui se lève
s'élève
ce qui se tend
s'étend

le dire
de l'enfant
est un rire

jamais
le vide
ne s'essouffle

an emptiness
that cannot be
breathless

inside it
a child
laughing eternally

the mirthful stars
spilling from his mouth
joyful cosmos

gathered in
God's embrace
clapping hands

vide sans fin
souffle infini

rire éternel du
one hand clapping

« Laissez venir à moi
les petits enfants »

how close children are
to divinity

so close
they may be

what God
might be

were he
to step

right from air
into light

but light
invisible

l'enfance est tout
paradis perdu
temps retrouvé

vieil océan
usque ad mare

je te salue
Marie

the air fell open
and in the voices of children
the first trees arose
virgin songs of birds
filling the air
of paradise reborn
in time again

le mystère n'a pas de contours
il est mouvement
rythme spirituel

dans la grande indifférence
de l'univers
la gratuité apparaît

c'est une grâce

the slow appearance
of the sun at dawn
shyly resting

horizons may disappear
and so the sun
but music will take it up

without thought
a music long forgotten
that leaves the birds baffled

qui parle
quand il n'y a que silence ?

les oiseaux se perdent-ils
dans les feuilles ?

le soleil
occupe l'espace
mais le tempo
est le temps mesuré

music that
can only hear itself
when time is kept
unlike the time we know

that no pendulum can seize
but just the soul's dancing
where silence hides
with unseen birds

le silence est toujours en place
il va et vient au rythme du temps
il mesure ce qui le précède
âme indivisible

time is the shade
of slow breathing
that measures the life
of each soul

crossing to the other shore
acquiring a new rhythm

ni son ni silence
exubérance contenue
le poète vogue
démesurément
sur la StylisStyx
un coup d'âme à la fois

sipping the strange waters
and sensing an unknown moon
rise briefly on your tongue

where a new cosmos comes
momentarily into being
reshaping the universe

dis ce qui passe
muet
entre les mots

délie la langue
qui prononce l'être
de l'univers

O speechless word
unheard
between the lines

no pentecostal
series of cries
fell so into the cosmos
calling out
among the planets

langue de feu
langue de foi
langue de joie
venez taire
le babil de Babel

ayez la gravité des astres
qui œuvrent en silence
depuis le début en leur fin